# The Terror Disease

Helen Sullivan

# DEDICATION

To all those who have ever experienced Terror
and to their loved ones

# INTRODUCTION

Born to Irish parents, I was the oldest of four children, with one sister and two brothers. Home was a place where I was made to repress feelings and speech. I was a sad and angry child. My mother was oblivious and felt women should be accommodating to make the men comfortable. I grew tall and matured physically, but the sad and angry little girl continued to run my life.

My heroes were cowboys, doctors, lawyers, and professional businessmen, but I felt that my own prospects were very limited. Upon graduating from high school, I thought the only options open to me were working at the phone company or becoming a nurse, teacher, or secretary. I attended college for two years, where I majored in Business Education. I left school and went to work because I could not bear the thought of standing in front of a class for practice teaching. Had I dared to be different, I would have pursued a career in business because I did have an aptitude for math.

I married and had three children. I had always fantasized that being a mother would fill the void I felt within, but that never happened. My husband was an educated man but felt that mothers were inconsequential and children a nuisance. Anti-feminism was not uncommon in Irish Catholic communities; men were put on a pedestal and women were subservient, even if the mothers were domineering. My husband abandoned us after our third child was born, and I was hospitalized with extreme depression and chronic anxiety. Withdrawing from the world only made matters worse. Anger, hopelessness, and feelings of terror increased. I was advised to live on disability. I was so disillusioned and weak.

When the time came for my children to go to college, they were embarrassed and angry that I was not able to help them with their college expenses. In fact, my youngest son told me how embarrassing it was to say on his financial aid application, "Mother's Occupation: disabled/homemaker." Yet when I tried to better myself by returning to school in my forties, my mother remarked: "you are making a fool of yourself going to college."

Reading Natalie Goldberg's *Writing Down to the Bones* emboldened me to put my experience into words. In her book she talks about tapping one's inner resources, energy, and spontaneity and letting go with zest and enthusiasm. The chapter about life and not wanting to die is truly inspirational. She discusses how one can look at one's roots and get real therapeutic results by writing from the heart and letting thoughts and feelings flow.

The book you now hold is the result of exploring my own roots and expressing myself in poetic form. It shows the raw terror and despair I have experienced, but now in my eighth decade I can say that God has been faithful. I find that prayers, faith, friends, and family give me reason to go on.

Helen Sullivan
August, 2018

# THE TERROR DISEASE

There is a nightmare
which most people
won't believe—In fact
most readers would
suspect a case of
insanity.

It happened when
I was a child
the fear raised
a curse on me
and took away
my liberty—but
I knew it
was a sickness
that later spoiled
my life.

All my life it
would come and
go and I found
ways to appear
with a normalcy.

1

At the age of twenty-six
it shook all my
body members
so fiercely that the
pain I knew
came from
my brain and
not from all the
people around me.

No one ever knew
how sad and scared
I was that it
would be the death
of me.

I longed for love
understanding
I knew it could
help but not cure
the anguish inside of
me.

I knew I must
see an expert
at the age of
twenty-six.
I labored over
each breath I
took and even
felt unable to
take a sip of
tea.

All was "unreal"
around me
It seemed like
I was a murderer
I felt God made
me the freakiest
being from all
eternity but I
tried to persevere
because of
the God-fearing
part of me.

I saw the chief
psychiatrist one
sunny May morn
he looked very
sternly at me.

I knew I had
to tell him
I had lost control—
the story of my disease.
But after three
years, twice a
week I visited
him—for three
months during
a crisis, I
saw him
each day—my
faith in him
was dying like

the plant with
no water to drink.

I reflected on his
therapy:
Mothers were the
cause of such tragedy,
Children were my
problem because
I carried an angry
child in me
He ruled my life
for many years
and made me
feel great woe.
I worked so
hard to learn
from him but
he did not know
the makings of
me.

I was angry at
him, saw no
excuse for his
cruelty—I
was an object
in his laboratory.

I felt I failed
and deserved to
die because
he was rude to

me. He knew
I worked and did my
best to be an independent woman.

I know I did my
best—but
it had been
to no avail
and only done
me harm—I
felt like a
rotten snake
and that I
must crawl
on the ground.
My legs were
rubbery each
long day and
would hardly
carry me.

I want to forgive
the man—I know
he didn't understand.
His training was
stern and orthodox.

My brain was mangled
tired and worn
and maybe I'll never
understand the
SHOCK it was
to me.

All my life I
gave each soul
the benefit of
the doubt!
I was completely
unaware till
then that such
an important man
felt it was okay
to forget about
another human
being's feelings.

I know feelings
mean so much.
They are crucial
in every life.

Once again it
was a SHOCK
the stupor hasn't ended.
The man I opened my soul to
said a suicide I'd be.

I married at age 22
with hope flickering in my
heart
A child I soon was
expecting.
The expecting father, my best
friend I believed,
would be a strength
that would give love

and together I
believed we would
love each other dearly
and raise our
children with tender
care and dignity.

What happened however
was so tragic
my big belly made him
angry
He hated babies and
children I learned
because they were
not thirty-three.

His anger at a
hungry babe
A babe who wanted
to romp and play
caused him to
hate the fools
he believed—that
was to be the kids
and me.

So battered, harassed
scorned and
broken—his
family's hearts were
torn with grief.

My limited phobias

grew and grew
I felt the need
to avoid people
places and things
the terror sickness
put me in a
different world—a
kind of insanity
where nightmares
confusion, terror
fear, extreme
sadness, a racing
heart, a gasp for
breath made
me a walking zombie.

Often I was extremely faint
The terror obsessions
haunted me
I believed I could
kill

The pain of my
mind and crazy
beliefs—made me
a vegetable,
that was rotted with
the terror disease.

Folks hate one
with the terror disease.
They believe they are
nothing—selfish

beings who are
selfish, demonic beings.

My nausea, stupor
and panic attacks
have made
me a desperate
agitated seemingly
like mad dog

Control of will, goals
and becoming
a comfortable
effective being
fly away with
my good spirit and
rationality.

I've been brave
taking risks constantly
I leave my bed
with hope of a
healing for me.
But sorrow for
twenty-five years of
working on the
terror disease
I have received
no victory.

I cannot tell the
grief when spoken to

## The Terror Disease

It's in my mind
when asked
but I can't
communicate or
explain this
killer of a disease.

The sickness is in
my gut
and shakes my
brain, bowels and
every body member
I pray to God
for rest to come
because my body
mind and soul
are exhausted
because there is
a big gap between
other souls and me.

I want a day of peace
where my emotions
will let me
be
a person who
belongs to the
world of normalcy.

I cannot work
I cannot play
the energy and

breath have
left me.
the light hurts my eyes
I gasp for air
each and every
day as I try
to be a friendly
kind friend to all.

But I have the
primitive drive
in me
It has made
a scared and
running rabbit of me.

I never met
another with
the terror disease
but I long to know
if anyone could
grasp this and
understand this
sickness in me.

I am dying and
may not be any more
if I cannot have
my right mind
and know and love
the places I may be.

God help me have
the courage to bear
and let me know
you care
let me praise and thank
let me feel
relief and comfortable be
So that I may
know sleep and energy.

My God I'm lonely,
I've been rejected
and hurt.
I'm in a maze
and daze
but help me
to continue my
search for
the answer and
cure for the
terror disease,
and copy like a living normal woman.

The people judge
and won't listen
They can't respect
they can't believe
and are not
willing to be
receptive and open
their hearts to a
person with the

terror disease.

The people consider
them crazy,
Treat them as
worthless and
inadequate.

Even doctors and lawyers
won't admit there
is a terror disease.
But it is real
I know this truth

Again I say something sets
the terror off
Alcohol and medicine
are considered the
terror disease
but I say no
the pain of fight
or flight can
come suddenly or
be anticipatory

This pain is excruciating
it is not mere
depression or normal
apprehension.
It makes one's head
kill
If the sufferer

screams he will
be labeled crazy.

So I can only speak
for myself
and say the
pain, disorientation,
guilt and anguish
would leave me no
choice but to kill
myself if it were
not for love, and
chemical drugs.

The unbearable pain
that might be worse
is having one's flesh
burned.

Likened to being
cremated alive
would not the
victim wish for
death.

And so too the
terror disease
kills.

To those who have
a slight degree
of the terror

disease—Get
HELP or you may
die.

The terror disease
can grow
and paralyze heart,
mind, soul, blood
vessels and be fatal.

And if not taken care
of the terror
disease can cause
a loss of control.
The brain is fuzzy
I know I can't think
and feel terrified
because I have to
sweat blood to know
who I am, where
I am---it is
mortifying to lose
one's sense of reality.

It's like a paralysis of
the brain—there is
no conscious control
in sight.

It's similar to
the night terror a
child has

which awakens
the child screaming.

It takes a while for
the fear to subside
and a sense of
reality to return.

Once again it is like
a nightmare
but it occurs when
one is awake.

Fainting, sweating,
nausea, incontinence,
stupor, collapse
are me during
each terror disease
attack.

It has taken my
strength
it knocks me out
I am unable to
speak
I feel so exhausted
when attacks are over—and restless
too
that I cannot
have interest in
my surroundings.

My heart struggles
to pump
I get so tired
when the TERROR
subsides

Sleep often
comes—and
does give the
body rest.
The rest is needed
to save sanity.

Physical and emotional
stress are
characteristic of the TERROR
disease. They make it
more agonizing.
My tolerance is low
It is work to get
thru a day.

I'm hurt, scared
and lonely because
the TERROR
DISEASE ravages
my mind and
body each day
The terror disease
took my
choices away.
It took my attitude

strength and will.

It makes me bitter
at times,
angry and resentful,
jealous and
cruel, hostile
and mean.
I must watch it!
It takes much effort
not to blame others.

And too with the terror
disease and the
accompanying depression
it's hard to think
rationally.
Terror fills my heart that
I'll land back in an insane
asylum or on the streets.

The Terror disease
is like the angry sea
it tosses and turns and
teases the drowning
victim and all the
victim can do
is try to stay
above the raging
waters—try to
breathe and remain
alive.

There's an angry monster
in the sea
it's like the one
inside of me
It is eating me alive
and all I can do
is fight and fight
to be set free.

And the monster
tells me stay away
from the human beings
the ugly blood pussy
sores are
disgusting.
Others must not
know they're there
or I'll die because
I'll be ousted
from society.
My kind of leprosy
is eating from
within—and so
I fool the people
at times and
appear to be a
responsible person with
dignity.

The educated and professionals
don't know about this disease
After employers by the

hundreds rejected me
I went to school to
make something of me

I did not learn about
me
and I'm angry and sad
I made a fool of
myself

I earned some degrees
but it was so hard
What hurt the most was
the mental health
teachers slighted
offended and rejected
me.

It struck me
as absurd
that those professed
as healers of mind
could hate and turn
their backs on me.

And at the same time
they taught the students
to be objective and
unjudgmental.